THE ANNOUNCER OF DESTINY

THE ANNOUNCER OF DESTINY

Joycelyn Dankwa

authorHOUSE®

AuthorHouse™
1663 Liberty Drive
Bloomington, IN 47403
www.authorhouse.com
Phone: 1-800-839-8640

Published by AuthorHouse   10/23/2012

ISBN: 978-1-4772-3963-6 (sc)
ISBN: 978-1-4772-4169-1 (e)

Library of Congress Control Number: 2012919885

Any people depicted in stock imagery provided by Thinkstock are models, and such images are being used for illustrative purposes only.
Certain stock imagery © Thinkstock.

This book is printed on acid-free paper.

Because of the dynamic nature of the Internet, any web addresses or links contained in this book may have changed since publication and may no longer be valid. The views expressed in this work are solely those of the author and do not necessarily reflect the views of the publisher, and the publisher hereby disclaims any responsibility for them.

Scripture taken from the Holy Bible, NEW INTERNATIONAL VERSION®. Copyright © 1973, 1978, 1984, 2011 by Biblica, Inc. All rights reserved worldwide. Used by permission.

NEW INTERNATIONAL VERSION® and NIV® are registered trademarks of Biblica, Inc. Use of either trademark for the offering of goods or services requires the prior written consent of Biblica US, Inc.

Contents

To my precious two boys: Bentley and Ephraim

You have been so understanding, supportive, and friendly. I am grateful to God that you appreciate His faithfulness in our lives. May you grow to become what God created you for.

I love you dearly, My sons

INTRODUCTION

We have all listened to an announcer at one time or another. It could be in person or through the media. In whatever situation you might have experienced an announcement being made, you will agree with me that it was meant to pass across important information. There is no reason for an announcement if there is no information to be passed across.

You may not have to do anything in particular or take any immediate step after the announcement has been made, but the information released nonetheless has a purpose. The purpose is to introduce something to you.

I had studied the several passages I will be using in this book a couple of times before now, but as I was studying them recently something that goes beyond information jumped at me, and it amazes me how important a role the announcer is meant to play in the life of an individual. Just as an announcer is not expected to get on the stage or screen without something concrete and tangible to say, so also have I come to discover that God does not place an announcer in and around our lives for no reason. The announcer is there for a purpose, and the purpose must be activated before destiny is fulfilled.

By virtue of revelational knowledge, I came to realize that destiny could be dormant until the announcer assigned by God takes his or her rightful place. The same place, the same issue that had been treated with levity or overlooked becomes celebrated once the announcer begins to perform his or her duty.

My passionate and ultimate desire is to *push* us into action, so as to prayerfully discover our destiny announcers. Even if we don't discover them, once they take up their expected position and carry out their assignment, the life ahead of us becomes easier, and the same place we were once tolerated becomes the place where we are celebrated.

Based on what the Lord had shown to me before now, you will discover how possible it is to grow from *nothing* to *something*, from *zero* to a *hero,* and from a liability to a celebrity with the help of the announcer.

May the Lord propel your destiny announcer to take it up as a duty to knock on the necessary door that will create an identity for you, so that you will move from the shameful stage of being a nonentity.

I can't stop thanking God for releasing this revelation to me. I'm ever grateful for His love and impartiality.

CHAPTER ONE

EVERYBODY NEEDS AN ANNOUNCER

Did I remember to mention while writing the introduction that everybody needs an announcer? Maybe it escaped my mind. However, it is a very crucial point to be emphasized and stressed that we all need somebody to announce us. Apart from the fact that it is not very honourable for you to announce yourself; people may in fact even dislike you for doing so. Even worse, the truth of the matter is that you may not have an opportunity to announce yourself, and even if you do have that opportunity, you may be treated as a liar.

There is always a platform for an announcer. It doesn't just come to pass that the announcer begins the announcement for no reason. Either there is a time to do so, or one thing leads to another. Ninety-nine per cent of the time when your destiny needs to be announced, you are not in a position to do so. Even if you are physically present in or around the venue, you are not asked. It makes more sense if somebody else comes up with what you are made of. It is more acceptable and will be embraced more than if you had presented it yourself. People are quick to judge you as being proud if you are the one announcing yourself.

> Let another man praise you, and not your own mouth, stranger, and not your own lips. (Proverbs 27: 2)

You can't hide who you are for long; whether you are good or bad. It becomes very clear to people within a twinkle of an eye. I always say being a hypocrite is a waste of time, because it will not be long before people know who you are. No matter how long you try to hide who you are from people, it should not surprise you that the people you don't even expect are able to write an epistle about who you are when an opportunity presents itself. Sometimes, or even many times, the opportunity you have been waiting for comes unannounced, but the discerning announcer assigned for your destiny picks the code immediately to announce you. If your destiny announcer gets the golden and rare opportunity today and he or she begins to say some things about you, do you think people will agree with what he or she is saying? Do you think that if he or she is against you, there will be people to stand up to defend you? Who are you? Maybe you don't even know yourself. Wait until someone begins to talk about you, and watch the response of others.

> A man is valued by what others say of him. (Proverbs 27: 21b)

The duty of an announcer of destiny is to say things about you that will propagate you and your destiny. Once your destiny announcer takes up his or her duty, you can be sure that something is about to happen. The arrival of your destiny announcer precedes that of you, the owner or carrier of the destiny. You are not completely released to function until your destiny announcer has finished his or her brief duty about you and your destiny.

Do you know that Jesus Christ Himself needed an announcer of destiny? John the Baptist was His destiny announcer. Actually, the main purpose of John's arrival on earth before Jesus Christ was to announce His destiny. Every other thing that John did was secondary. His primary assignment was to be an announcer for the arrival of Jesus' destiny on earth.

There is a purpose for every conception. No matter what circumstances surround your conception or birth, you must never forget that God's omnipresent power was part of it from the beginning. Even if everything around you seems contrary to the prophesy, you can be assured today by this revelation that your purpose shall be fulfilled no matter what.

But the angel said to him, do not be afraid, Zacharias, for your prayer is heard; and your wife Elizabeth will bear you a son, and you shall call his name John. And you will have joy and gladness, and many will rejoice at his birth. For he will be great in the sight of the Lord, and shall drink neither wine nor strong drink. He will also be filled with the Holy Spirit, even from his mother's womb. And he will turn many of the children of Israel to the Lord their God. He will also go before Him in the spirit and power of Elijah, to turn the hearts of the fathers to the children, and the disobedient to the wisdom of the just, to make ready a people prepared for the Lord. (Luke 1: 13-17)

If God could deliberately create a whole human being to go before Christ and announce Him, then the office of destiny announcer is not to be taken for granted. God is always true to His words. The moment John the Baptist was born, the Lord filled his father, Zacharias with the Holy Spirit, and he started to prophesy. Here is one of the crucial things he said while declaring the purpose of John, his son:

And you, child, will be called the prophet of the Highest, for you will go before the face of the Lord to prepare His ways, to give knowledge of salvation to His people by the remission of their sins, through the tender mercy of our God, with which the Dayspring from on high has visited us. To give light to those who sit in darkness and the shadow of death, to guide our feet into the way of peace. (Luke 1: 76)

If God could feel the need for an announcer for Jesus' arrival, and He filled this need with John the Baptist who arrived ahead of Jesus, then the office of the announcer cannot be over-emphasized. Realize that Jesus was not an ordinary being like us, and yet God felt He needed someone to announce His destiny. This is an indication that everyone who loves his or her destiny must arise now and fight the good fight.

There is something in you that somebody needs to announce for the entire world to embrace. What is that thing? Have you discovered it yet? You must never take it for granted. You need to celebrate it and love it with all your heart. The passion with which you embrace the destiny may determine the steps that your destiny announcer takes.

For the purpose of emphasis, let me stress that you don't necessarily have to be around before your destiny announcer takes up his or her duty. Jesus Christ was not even born when the prophecies had gone ahead of Him when John the Baptist was born.

David was still in the wilderness when the announcer of his destiny was quickened by the spirit of the Lord to announce him for the assignment ahead of him. Shortly after David had been anointed by the prophet, he needed a connection that would open the doors of the palace to him. Nothing could bring him to the palace except divine intervention. His father's status was very low and unrecognized in Israel. He did not even realize that he needed to be connected to the palace.

What about Saul, who went out as an obedient son to look for his for father's donkey? Meanwhile God had spoken to Samuel, telling him to anoint him king over Israel. His family was the smallest in Israel and he was the youngest among his family. The loss of a donkey leaves him thrown.

While he was busy with his duty in the wilderness, the announcer had taken up his duty of helping David to activate his destiny. In other words, it was time for the announcer to fulfil the reason why he was in the palace as a servant. Things don't just happen. There is always a reason for everything that happens. The moment the platform was ready for David, the servant in the palace just started the announcement without any restrictions or hindrances.

> So Saul said to his servants, provide me now a man who can play well, and bring him to me. Then one of the servants answered and said:

(And then the announcement begins.)

> Look, I have seen a son of Jesse the Bethlehemite, who is skilful in playing, a mighty man of valour, a man of war, prudent in speech, and a handsome person; and the Lord is with him. (1 Samuel 16: 17-18)

The above announcement was all that David needed for his destiny to be unfolded. The moment the announcer performed his duty of announcing David's destiny, his destiny began to take the necessary shape. The king immediately took action based on the announcement made

> Therefore Saul sent messengers to Jesse and said,
> send me your son David who is with the sheep.
> (1 Samuel 16: 19)

Before the announcer of destiny took up his role in the life of David, the king did not know who David was. He didn't even know Jesse either. They were not prominent. Even though the king did not know David, God knew him, and He created him with an enviable destiny.

The duty of the announcer of destiny is usually not a prolonged one; generally, it is very brief and direct. However, nothing happens until the announcer takes up his or her role. The same David who had been in the wilderness without anyone noticing became the celebrity of the year the moment his announcer of destiny took up his role.

Not long after the announcement, there was an invitation from the palace, and before long David became the amour bearer to the king, which was in those days a great office. He also became the musical instrumentalist to the king. He held the key to quenching the demonic spirit tormenting the king. No one would have known all of these things if David's destiny announcer had not come up to the stage.

By reason of this announcement as well, David's fighting skill was enhanced, and he killed Goliath, whom no one had been able to kill for so long. David's ultimate destiny was to become the king of Israel, but he had to start from somewhere. His starting point was when the announcer felt inspired to speak about him. Don't you think you should take the next step at this point?

Next step: praying point:

"O Lord, please, inspire my announcer of destiny to be quickened to take the right step that will lead me to the place of destiny assigned for me in Jesus' name."

CHAPTER TWO

HAVE YOU GOT AN ATTITUDE?

You must have heard it said of someone before: "Oh, she's got an attitude" or "He has this offensive attitude." I don't think you need a prophet to tell you that your attitude, as it is generally said, determines your altitude. In other words, having an attitude, as used in this context, is negative. A wrong attitude turns the back of your destiny announcer towards you and turns his or her face in another direction. To be able to enjoy favour, you have to be in the sight of your destiny announcer and not at the back. Anything that makes your destiny announcer turn his or her face away from you is not a good sign.

Several things could bring about a bad attitude in the life of any human being. Nothing locks the door against one's destiny faster than a bad attitude. Some of these factors include pride, false accusation, distrust, misconception, etc.

Picking distrust and false accusation as an example, Ishboseth, a surviving son of Saul, had a very bad attitude towards somebody who would have helped his destiny. He distrusted Abner, who had always supported his father and had been on the side of their family for so long. Despite the fact that Abner and everyone around knew that the kingdom had been taken away from Saul and given to David, he still maintained his loyalty until Ishboseth came up with an attitude of distrust and false accusation.

> Now it was so, while there was war between the house of Saul and the house of David, that Abner was strengthening his hold on the house of Saul. And Saul had a concubine whose name was Rizpah, the daughter of Aiah. <u>So Ishboseth said to Abner, Why have you gone into my father's concubine?</u> (2 Samuel 3: 6-7)

The moment Ishboseth distrusted Abner, who was meant to help him with his destiny, he lost the chance of progression. Instead of moving forward, he started to regress. Nothing makes regression easier and faster than losing favour with the one who is meant to be a helper or announcer of destiny. If your announcer of destiny gets angry with you, or if he turns against you, be ready for a very hard time. That was what happened in the life of Ishboseth. The moment he distrusted Abner and accused him wrongly, he lost the battle of survival and progress. He misplaced the code to his success and had nothing left to fight for. Abner became very angry, and he turned against Ishboseth, the same prince for whom he was once ready to stick out his neck

Then Abner became very angry at the words of Ishboseth, and said, Am I a dog's head that belongs to Judah? Today I show loyalty to the house of Saul your father, to his brothers, and to his friends, and have not delivered you into the hand of David; and you charge me today with a fault concerning this woman? May God do so to Abner, and more also, if I do not do for David as the Lord has sworn to him—to transfer the kingdom from the house of Saul, and set up the throne of David over Israel and over Judah from Dan to Beersheba. (2 Samuel 3: 8-10)

The false accusation and distrust that Ishboseth displayed towards the man who was meant to be his destiny announcer pulled him off track. He missed his way and could no longer trace his steps back. Before he knew what was happening, Abner had already diverted his loyalty from the entire family of Saul. He felt his loyalty was being wasted, and he diverted it to where it was going to be appreciated. He felt that David, whom the Lord Himself had chosen, should rule instead of the ungrateful Ishboseth. Of course, Ishboseth could not answer Abner a word, because he had just lost a great battle. He disregarded his announcer of destiny, and before long Abner had shifted his base to David's camp.

Then Abner sent messengers on his behalf to David, saying, Whose is the land? Saying also, Make covenant with me, and indeed my hand shall be with you to bring all Israel to you. And David said, Good, I will make a covenant with you (2 Samuel 3: 12-13a)

Remembering how powerful Abner was, David agreed to make a covenant with him. He knew that Abner was definitely going to be a plus to his destiny. Instead of disregarding his offer, he quickly embraced it, and within the twinkling of an eye, things started taking shape beyond expectations.

Initially David placed a very strong demand on Abner to be sure of his commitment and change of loyalty. David asked for his wife Michal, whose dowry he paid with one hundred foreskins of the Philistines. There was nothing to drag or prolong. All that Abner needed to do was to command Paltiel, her second husband whom her father, Saul gave her just to pass a message of disapproval, disrespect and rejection to David with the instruction from Abner, Ishboseth was compelled to command Paltiel to release Michal. Whether he liked it or not, he had to do so.

> But one thing I require of you: you shall not see my face unless you first bring Michal, Saul's daughter, when you come to see my face. So David sent messengers to Ishboseth, Saul's son, saying, Give me my wife, Michal, whom I betrothed to myself for a hundred foreskins of the Philistines. And Ishboseth sent and took her from her husband, from Paltiel the son of Laish. Then her husband went along with her to Bahurim, weeping behind her. <u>So Abner said to him, Go return! And he returned. (</u>2 Samuel 3: 13b)

Sometimes helpers of destiny that are divinely arranged to announce and introduce us to the next level are very powerful, influential, and great in status. And sometimes they are not. You must be very careful not to make the mistake of disregarding the people God is bringing your way. Do not think too highly of yourself. Ishboseth definitely thought too highly of himself, and he allowed his position as the prince to overshadow his reason. He became prideful, thinking that Abner was only one of his father's officers. He didn't realize how powerful and influential Abner was until he lost his friendship with him. He traded the favour he had with his announcer of destiny for mere accusation and distrust. He only realized how powerful Abner was after he had misbehaved towards him. Not only did Abner command him to bring Michal back to David, he also commanded Paltiel, Michal's second husband, to return, and he didn't argue with him.

Abner's strength, which he might have used to help Ishboseth, extended far beyond the four walls of the palace. It reached virtually every corner of the city and the entire country. That was what informed Abner's communication with the elders of Israel and with Benjamin and David himself. His influence allowed him to enjoy a lovely feast with David when he paid him a visit at Hebron.

> Now Abner had communicated with the elders of Israel, saying, In time past you were seeking David to be king over you. Now then, do it! For the Lord has spoken of David, saying, By the hand of my servant David I will save my people Israel from the hand of the Philistines and the hand of all their enemies. And Abner spoke in

> the hearing of Benjamin. Then Abner also went
> to speak in the hearing of David in Hebron. <u>And
> David made a feast for Abner</u> and the men who
> were with him. Then Abner said to David, I will
> arise and go, and gather all Israel to my lord the
> king, that they may make a covenant with you,
> and that you may reign over all that your heart
> desires. So David sent Abner away, and he went
> in peace. (2 Samuel 3: 17)

The best thing is never to fall into an error. Once an error has been made, it keeps opening more doors for dangers and disasters. Bad attitude is an error. It got to a point that Ishboseth's mistake in wrongly accusing Abner led to Abner's death because it made him go to King David's territory. David did not kill him, Joab did, and since Abner had died, it opened an evil door for Ishboseth as well—the door of death. He got murdered in his own room on his own bed by mere men just because Abner, his announcer of destiny, had died a very cheap death.

Until Abner's death, nobody was strong enough to harass Ishboseth. The fear of Abner gripped everyone around Ishboseth. Not even David attempted to rule over Israel by force. He only became king in Hebron and not the whole of Israel until Abner came around to surrender his commitment and loyalty. Abner was a great warrior and a well-respected officer; his death came so cheaply because Ishboseth's bad attitude pushed him where he shouldn't have gone. When Joab heard that he paid David a visit and left peacefully, Joab could not believe it. He capitalized on that friendship and executed Abner, who had been a terror to them all this while.

The exit of an announcer of destiny may mean that the destiny being announced or that is expected to be announced is also expiring. In the case of Ishboseth, David could have remained in Hebron for more than the seven years and six months that he reigned there, but the expiration of Ishboseth's destiny, which became apparent when Abner died, led David to reign over all of Israel, and that was because Ishboseth himself had died.

Significantly, Ishboseth's head, which was brought by the wicked men who killed him to seek David's favour, was buried in the same tomb with Abner in Hebron. There was a split in Ishboseth's destiny: there arose an embarrassing break in his purpose the moment he came up with a bad attitude that pushed away his announcer of destiny.

Another outstanding scenario will help us act properly at all times and circumstances, for you may not know who your announcer of destiny is.

Abraham sent his servant to go and find a wife for Isaac. The Bible says that when the servant finished praying, Rebekah came out to draw water, and he asked her for water. Gen 24: 19-20 says that she quickly emptied her jar into the trough and ran back and forth until they all had enough. Look at verse 21: "Without saying a word, the man watched her closely to learn whether or not the Lord had made his journey successful." What a character! Rebekah did not know who the man was, but she showed the right attitude of service, and she was announced to her destiny. No wonder it is written "A man's gift makes a room a home."

Now, have you got attitude? Good or bad? You are in the best position to answer.

CHAPTER THREE

RIGHT TIMING FOR THE ANNOUNCEMENT

Our God is very organized and orderly. He has His own timing for everything. When the time is ripe, it becomes the right timing for the manifestation of His purpose. The person prepared for the announcement then comes up when the stage or the screen is ready. In the case of John the Baptist, he had to wait for the day of manifestation according to God's divine calendar.

> So the child grew and became strong in spirit, and was in the deserts till the day of his manifestation to Israel. (Luke 1: 80)

You cannot manifest until the assigned time for your destiny. In other words, there is a right timing that must be discovered by whoever has been assigned to bring you to the stage of advancement. The moment God is ready for you, He arranges everything to fall into place. While God is preparing the destiny carrier for manifestation, He is also preparing the announcer of destiny for the right timing to make the announcement. The main purpose of John the Baptist's existence was to announce the destiny of Jesus. Even the announcer needs preparation and right timing before manifestation.

The same John the Baptist whose duty was to announce and who had been in the wilderness, was the one who was all over the city the moment his time of manifestation came. He didn't have to put pressure on God to let him manifest. There is always a right timing to connect yourself with if you are moving in the schemes of God. You are never too late or too early if it is God that is in charge, He leads you to the right place and the right people. He quickens the spirit of the announcer to speak out appropriately. Once the timing is right and the announcer speaks forth as prompted, action begins accordingly.

The prophet Nathan saw something that nobody else saw. He was Solomon's announcer of destiny; he saw his beautiful destiny ahead of time. Someone else was bragging about the seat that belonged to Solomon. When the right timing came, the announcer stepped in and announced the destiny. It was a vulnerable time for King David. He had been exhausted and weak. When Adonijah saw that the king was exhausted, he exalted himself falsely.

Now King David was old, advanced in years; and they put covers on him, but he could not get warm. Therefore his servants said to him, let a young woman, a virgin, be sought for our Lord the King, and let her care for him; and let her lie in your bosom, that our Lord the king may be warm. So they sought for a lovely young woman throughout all the territory of Israel, and found Abishhag the Shunamite and brought her to the king. The young woman was very lovely; and she cared for the king, and served him; but the king did not know her. (1 Kings 1: 1)

The situation of King David was bad to the point that even if he thought about his kingdom, he surely did not have enough strength to carry out anything. Whatever made King David un able to "know" the young beautiful virgin on his bosom was far above the ordinary. It was this vulnerability that Adonijah capitalized on. Not realizing that it was not his destiny to become the next king, he tried to announce himself. You cannot be announced if God does not announce you. He is the one to send an announcer to you to help you activate your destiny.

Let another man praise you, and not your own mouth. (Proverbs 27: 2a)

The man who will praise you will be your God-sent announcer. If you try to praise or announce yourself, you may end up being disgraced like Adonijah. He joined hands with the wrong set of people to occupy a place that didn't belong to him. At the end of the story, he had to disgracefully vacate the throne that was never his.

Then Adonijah the son of Haggith exalted himself, saying, I will be king, and he prepared for himself chariots and horsemen, and fifty men to run before him. And his father had not rebuked him at any time by saying, Why have you done so? He was also very good-looking. His mother had borne him after Absalom. Then he conferred with Joab the son of Zeruiah and with Abiathar the priest, and they followed and helped Adonijah. (1 Kings 1: 5)

If you are not helped by the Lord, you are not truly helped. There is nothing for you to receive unless it is given from the Lord. Anything a man or group of men may give you, it is only temporary if it is not from the Lord. Whatever the Lord gives is for ever. Unfortunately, Adonijah did not realize this truth. He assumed he was helped because he had mere men on his side. If God does not choose men to help you, their help cannot be permanent.

In spite of the sacrifices that Adonijah made, he still failed in his attempt to become the king all by himself. He had all his brothers on his side except Solomon, God's chosen king after their father David. He even had all the men of Judah and the king's servants with him, but because God was not with him, his camp was empty. He had men on his side all right, but none of them was his announcer of destiny.

But Zadok the priest, Benaiah the son of Jehoiada, Nathan the prophet, Shimei, Rei, and the mighty men who belonged to David were not with Adonijah. But Adonijah sacrificed sheep and oxen and fattened cattle by the stone of Zoheleth, which is by En Rogel; he also invited all his brothers, the king's sons, and all the men of Judah, the king's servants. But he did not invite Nathan the prophet, Benaiah, the mighty men, or Solomon his brother. (1 Kings 1: 8)

Sometimes, God will let the proud keep bragging and making unnecessary noise to the last drop of their strength. When they are not able to continue any longer, God begins to show forth His undeniable power. After Adonijah had exhausted his strength by sacrificing everything within his human capacity, God prompted Solomon's announcer of destiny, the respected prophet Nathan. The moment he felt quickened in his heart, he stood up for an uncommon action. He alone was more than the troop with Adonijah. His presence carried weight before King David. He was Solomon's announcer of destiny.

The interesting thing about the announcer of destiny is that God can decide to use anyone for this assignment. It may come in an unusual way or an unconventional manner. Even if Solomon had sensed that the throne belonged to him, he would never have calculated that the breakthrough could come through the prophet himself. The troop that Adonijah had behind him made the throne a scary place for Solomon to attempt, but God had a different plan.

Be very careful not to be rigid about anything in life. God may decide to come through for you in an unexpected way. As long as you know God is the one leading you, your safety is assured.

> So Nathan spoke to Bathsheba the mother of Solomon, saying, Have you not heard that Adonijah the son of Haggith has become king, and David our Lord does not know it? (1 Kings 1: 11)

Who would have believed from the way the above conversation started that it would have ended up positively? Had Bathsheba not been a very sensitive woman, she would have insulted the prophet or accused him of gossiping, and that would have sent Solomon's announcer of destiny away forever. You can never be right unless you are sensitive in the spirit. A conversation starting that way under other circumstances could land you into trouble unless you are guided to proceed. Anyway, Bathsheba responded by paying attention.

> Come, please, let me now give you advice, that you may save your own life and the life of your own son Solomon. Go immediately to King David and say to him, Did you not, my lord O king, swear to your maid servant, saying, Assuredly your son Solomon shall reign after me, and he shall sit on my throne? Why then has Adonijah become king? Then, while you are still talking there with the king, I also will come in after you and confirm your words. (1 Kings 1: 12-14)

Solomon had a double portion of announcers. His father's prophet was his destiny announcer, and so was his mother. Things might not have worked out if Bathsheba his mother had not caught the revelation. The moment the prophet Nathan said it, Bathsheba caught the idea and danced along.

> So Bathsheba went into the chamber to the king. Now the king was very old, and Abishag the Shunamite was serving the king. And Bathsheba bowed and did homage to the king. Then the king said, What is your wish? Then she said to him, My lord, you swore by the Lord your God to your maidservant, saying assuredly, Solomon your son shall reign after me, and he shall sit on my throne. So now, look! Adonijah has become king; and now, my lord the king, you did not know about it. He has sacrificed oxen and fattened cattle and sheep in abundance, and has invited all the sons of the king, Abiathar the priest, and Joab the commander of the army, but Solomon your servant he has not invited. And as for you, my lord, O king, the eyes of all Israel are on you that you should tell them who will sit on the throne of my lord the king after him. Otherwise it will happen, when my lord the king rests with his fathers, that I and my son Solomon will be counted as offenders. (1 Kings 1: 15-21)

If you read through Bathsheba's speech, you will notice that she went farther than the instructions she was given by the prophet. This was not only because she was Solomon's mother, it was mostly because she was Solomon's announcer of destiny. Not every mother is an announcer of destiny for their children, but if you are blessed to be divinely connected to your mother, it makes life easier for you. While Bathsheba was still speaking, the prophet Nathan fulfilled his promise by coming into the scene with grace.

> And just then, while she was still talking with the king, Nathan the prophet also came in. (1 Kings 1: 22)

What perfect timing—just when Bathsheba needed an additional approval before the final approval from the king. The respected prophet did not spare any words. He spoke gracefully to the king and the conclusion of the matter was that Solomon was enthroned. The moment the prophet Nathan announced Solomon's destiny, it became sanctioned with an authority that could not be questioned by anyone young or old. The final authority was what Solomon had on his side—the king—and he did not hesitate to release his authority after his announcers of destiny had performed their duties.

> And King David said, Call to me Zadok the priest, Nathan the prophet, and Benaiah the son of Jehoiada. So they came before the king. The king also said to them, Take with you the servants of your lord, and have Solomon my son ride on my own mule, and take him down to Gihon. There let Zadok the priest and Nathan the prophet anoint him king over Israel, and blow the horn and say, Long live king Solomon! Then you shall come up after him, and he shall come and sit on my throne and he shall be king in my

place. For I have appointed him to be ruler over
Israel and Judah. (1 Kings 1: 32-35)

Something miraculous happens the moment the
announcer of destiny takes up his or her assignment.
Until Solomon's announcer of destiny rose up to take
action, everything was dormant. This is traceable
to the fact that it was not yet the appointed time.
God's appointed time is the right time. It does not
come later; He is always on time. Pray that your
announcer of destiny does not miss God's prompting
and quickening. Imagine if the prophet Nathan had
ignored the prompting in his heart to speak on behalf
of Solomon, Adonijah would probably have remained
the king, and he would have been the wrong choice for
God's people. Your destiny announcer must speak!

CHAPTER FOUR

ARE YOU LOWLY IN STATE?

When the timing is right, no matter how lowly your state is, God remembers you. He knows your frame, and He is never going to let you be put to shame.

> Who remembered us in our lowly state.
> (Psalm 136: 23)

Solomon was down there in a very lowly state. There was no sign or clue that he was ever going to get to the throne. His mother was an illegal woman in the palace who had to hide her face for so long. However, when the right timing came for Solomon's destiny to be announced, the prophet Nathan felt prompted, and he did the unusual. Your level or your state does not matter. Once it is God's appointed time, He lifts you up without any consultation with human beings.

What a lowly state Solomon was in at the palace. His mother did not enter into the palace through the front door. She entered through the exit. Therefore she had no say in the affairs of the palace. She was like an outcast there. Not too many people reckoned with both the mother and the son. To everyone that loved King David, she was the one that made the king fall. Both Solomon and Bathsheba encountered ridicule and humiliation. They were both down there. When Adonijah exalted himself above God's platform for him, he invited every other son of the king except Solomon, because he was of no consequence to them in the palace.

> And Adonijah slew sheep and oxen and fat cattle by the stone of Zoheleth, which is by En Rogel, and called all his brethren the king's sons, and all the men of Judah the king's servants. But Nathan the prophet and Benaiah, and the mighty men, and Solomon his brother, he called not. (1 Kings 1: 9-10)

Despite the lowly state that Solomon was in with his mother, the Lord decided to elevate them because they were not far from where His grace was. He knew they were being humiliated, and He therefore elevated them. The same Solomon who was never heard or allowed to do anything significant became the king of Israel the moment his announcer of destiny had spoken.

If you check through your Bible, you will discover that nothing happened between the time that Solomon was named after birth until he was ready to be enthroned. Several events took place in Israel and Judah with not one reference to him or his mother Bathsheba because of the grief that Bathsheba's relationship with the king had caused the entire kingdom. The moment Solomon was born, it became a silent affair from that point on.

> Then David comforted Bathsheba his wife, went in to her and lay with her. So she bore a son, and he called his name Solomon. Now the Lord loved him. (2 Samuel 12: 23)

From birth till adulthood, there was no action in the physical realm, but in the spiritual realm, several things had happened. Before anything happens in the physical, it must first of all be settled in the spiritual. There was no controversy about the fact that the Lord loved Solomon specially. That still did not stop Him from keeping Solomon in a verylowly state until his time of manifestation. Solomon did not have to struggle, but God raised announcers of destiny for him and crowned their efforts with great success.

Before we could know what was happening, Solomon had been lifted from his lowly state to the highest state. A person who was more or less a nobody in the palace became the most important individual in the entire country. He became the first man to be reckoned with. What are you going through now? What exactly is happening in your life at the moment? Be assured that it is only for the time being. It is not going to remain negative for ever. You are coming up with great honour, like the Lord did for Solomon. God is ever mindful of your reproach. He is ever thinking of you.

Psalm 90: 50 says, "Remember, Lord, the reproach of your servants." All you need to do is to stay in tune with God as His servant. Don't move out of where He has placed you. Don't force your way out. Let Him be the one who will guide you out of your lowly state. His guiding hands are lifting hands. If He lifted Solomon from a nobody to a somebody, He will lift you up. Your enemies may be busy bragging somewhere because they think you are voiceless. However, there is a voice that can never be mistaken that God has put into somebody somewhere to announce your enthronement. After Solomon had been enthroned, there was an uproar in the city. They did not know that the same person they had despised had just been elevated. While your enemies are waiting for your disgrace, God is elevating you somewhere with grace. They heard about Solomon's advancement because another announcer of destiny was on duty.

> So Zadok the priest, Nathan the prophet, Benaiah the son of Jehoiada, the Cherethites, and the Pelethites went down and had Solomon ride on King David's mule, and took him to Gihon. Then Zadok the priest took a horn of oil from the tabernacle and anointed Solomon. And they blew the horn, and all the people said, Long live King Solomon. And all the people went up after him, and the people played the flutes and rejoiced with great joy, so that the earth seemed to split with their sound. Now

Adonijah and all the guests who were with him
heard it as they finished eating. And when Joab
heard the sound of the horn, he said, Why is
the city in such a noisy uproar? While he was
still speaking, there came Jonathan, the son of
Abiathar the priest. And Adonijah said to him,
Come in, for you are a prominent man, and
bring good news. Then Jonathan answered and
said to Adonijah, No! our lord King David has
made Solomon king. The king has sent with him
Zadok the priest, Nathan the prophet, Benaiah
the son of Jehoiada, the Cherethites, and the
Pelethites, and they have made him ride on the
king's mule. So Zadok the priest and Nathan
the prophet have anointed him king at Gihon;
and they have gone up from there rejoicing, so
that the city is in an uproar. This is the noise
that you have heard. (1 Kings 1: 38-45)

Solomon was so blessed and lifted from his lowly state
that God took the news of his enthronement into the
camp of his enemies by raising Jonathan the son of
Abiathar the priest as his announcer of destiny. The
essence of Jonathan's announcement was to put an
end to the evil rejoicing in the camp of the enemies.
The moment Solomon's destiny was announced, the
story changed at the camp of the enemies. They filed
themselves out one after the other. If your announcer
bring you out from your hidden place into limelight, you
could no longer be covered. The people that mattered
had gathered together with the King's authority and
nothing could be undone from what they had done
already.

Also Solomon sits on the throne of the kingdom. And moreover the King's servants have gone to bless our lord king David, saying, May God make the name of Solomon better than your name, and may He make his throne greater than your throne. Then the king bowed himself on the bed. Also the king said thus, Blessed be the Lord God of Israel, who has given one to sit on my throne this day while my eyes see it! So all the guests who were with Adonijah were afraid, and arose, and each one went his way. (1 Kings 1: 46)

No matter the number of people gathering against you, God is able to scatter them, and you will never see them anymore. Your lowly state is not your final state. No matter how long you have been there, you are only there temporarily. The moment God is ready to bring you to the limelight, He quickens the heart of your announcer of destiny, who takes up his duty without delay, and you are elevated to the highest level. Don't let your present lowly state determine your outlook to life. Get ready for where you are going, because it is an enviable place. Your announcer of destiny is commissioned already and your destiny is taking beautiful shape in Jesus' name.

CHAPTER FIVE

RECOGNISE YOUR ANNOUNCER

The issue of destiny announcer is a clear case of the manifestations of God's prerogative and sovereignty. Life is more spiritual than physical. It amazes me when people despise important spiritual matters. That is why God calls such as fools. Everyone is born with a talent and hidden potential. That potential when expressed is what lifts people up. That potential, the quality in you and outside of you is what your announcer helps you to announce. No matter how beautiful a woman is she will not marry herself the same thing goes for a bachelor. Whereas there are instances where two young people meet themselves but most times there are intermediaries that links them together. That is the case you see in the case of Rebecca and Isaac. Rebecca was a pretty woman, which is called charisma but she also has good character which help the announcer to recognize her. In Genesis chapter twenty-four we have the story where Abraham wants the best wife for his son Isaac. He was not interested in any woman but the best. In our time what Abraham was saying is that I want my daughter to marry a Christian. But we know that all Christians are not marriageable. Marriageable ones are home makers, people who have good spirit of hospitality. So the lead servant of Abraham made that prayer, anyone that will come and care for me and care for the animals and give us water to drink will be a good candidate and a good wife for Isaac. How do you recognize your announcer one of the ways is for you to just be a person of good character? Wherever you are your announcer will recognize you. No one chooses his announcer it is God's prerogative but you must recognize the person.

I remember the story of a young man in Nigeria. He wanted to be a taxi driver. A passion he developed by just watching a driver doing his job. But he went to school and had good grades in high school. He found a Laboratory Assistant job somewhere in Lagos, but he was wasting away. Where he was working another young man a Muslim saw his certificates and high grades and advised him to go to higher institution to better his lot. The Muslim friend went and got a form for higher school and eventually, this man attended that higher school and from there he went to university. Today instead of being a taxi driver he has a PhD in Chemical Engineering. He had the potential but he needed an announcer. An announcer is the person God has destined to discover your talent and position you in life. He was able to recognize his announcer and he grabbed it.

Let us look at the life of Joseph. How did he recognize his announcer? Joseph was endowed with the gift of dreams. He was a dreamer. That was a talent he discovered at a early stage. He developed that and became a dream interpreter. Many a times our announcers are not our friends. In Genesis thirty-seven the first levels of announcers of Joseph were his brother. They screamed—Here comes the dreamer! Though they meant it in a negative way they were the first to recognize his potential and greatness. Some of you reading this book, there are some people in your lives right now who are calling you names based on your potential and some in a sarcastic manner. Watch it, they are announcing you. Some of you by the way you debate they call you orators. Some of you the way you care they call you career and helpers. Some of you are brilliant and very good in science and they call you 'Engineer', 'Doctors', some of you are good in mathematics and they call you 'accountants' some of them are your announcers. They have recognized your gift and talents. Your gifts will make room for us.

Your announcer can only announce you they cannot destroy you! The brothers of Joseph sold him to slavery and took away the lovely coat of many colours that Jacob bought for him. Your announcer can take away what man has given to you they cannot take away what God has given to you. "The gifts and the calling of God is without repentance" Rom 11:29. Your announcer is there to announce you.

Joseph was falsely thrown to prison. He met his announcer in the prison. I pray for the reader of this book that you will meet your announcer whether in prison or in church or in school or in the work place.

Many people have met their announcer in the prison or unexpected places. They were going in wrong directions in life. They were drug addicts, womanizers, kidnappers, arsonist, fraudulent people and they were thrown into prison, and some people go to that place and preach to them and from there they embraced the gospel of Jesus and today they are Christians their lives are totally turn around. What is important is that you recognize your announcer.

Two people came to Joseph for interpretation of their dreams. After interpreting the dreams and one of them was favorably disposed Joseph said-

"But think on me when it shall be well with thee, and she's kindness, I pray thee, unto me, and make mention of me unto Pharaoh, and bring me out of this house. For indeed I was stolen away out of the land of the Hebrews: and here also have I done nothing that they should put me into the dungeon." Genesis 40:14-15.

Though this was a prisoner like him he did not look at him as a prisoner he saw the potential the man has the fact that he was walking in the presidency. Many of us also are not patient for our announcer to do his job. The Butler (cup bearer) forgot Joseph. The bible did not tell us more about Joseph within the two years when the Butler forgot him but I believe that Joseph must have been praying. It is not out of place to pray for God to bring to you your announcer. The bible is a practical book. Instead of living your life in mystery, complaining and grumbling pray that God will help you to recognize your announcer or vise-versa. Whether you recognize your announcer or your announcer recognizes you the most important thing is that you fulfill your purpose and fulfilling your purpose is tied to your announcer. Bear in mind that your announcer is simply your helper and promoter.

Let us look at one other bible character that also recognizes her announcer in a very peculiar way. The person in question is Ruth. Naomi was the mother in-law of Ruth. Naomi looked as a person that missed her purpose in life. Her life was miserable. So miserable that she herself was willing to change her name from Naomi (Sweet) to Mara (bitter) but all things worked together for good and her bitter story had a happy ending. Your life no matter how bitter it is now will become better.

In the book of Ruth chapter one Naomi and the husband Elimelech were hasty in taking decision. A little famine in the land of Jerusalem 'the land that flows with milk and honey 'drove them to the land of Moab where they met their waterloo. Naomi lost her husband and her two sons. She soon found out that the land of Canaan famine has disappeared and the rains were back. She just announced to her daughter in-laws her plans to go back and because they were Moabites she has no intension of going back to Canaan with them according to her she has nothing to offer Orpah or Ruth or both. As mentioned above your announcer just reveals who you are, your character. Your announcer does not determine who you are it revealed who you are. John the Baptist did not determine who Jesus was he just revealed his deity. When asked are you the Messiah he said no I am only baptizing people with water the Messiah does something much more he baptises with Holy Ghost Fire.

"And Ruth said, intreat me not to, leave thee,or to return from following after thee: for whither thou goest,I will go; and where thou lodgest, I will lodge: thy people shall be my people and thy God my God: where thou diest,will I die and there will I be buried: the Lord do so to me, and more also, if ought but death part thee and me."Ruth 1: 16-17.

With those few words she unknowinly recognized her announcer. There was nothing in Naomi that could have being a blessing to Ruth, she was a widow, penniless, childless and vulnerable, yet Ruth saw her as her destiny announcer and she followed through. Was it an easy route no, but the end showed that she made the choice of her life. Ruth the widow remarried Boaz, and gave birth to Obed, who gave birth to Jesse who became the father of David and through who's lineage Jesus Christ was born.

Let me help you to understand that the Holy Spirit is your helper who also will help you recognize your announcer. The Holy Spirit's desire and purpose is to help you not to hinder you.

"And I will pray the Father, and He will give you another Helper, that He may abide with you forever, even the Spirit of truth, whom the world cannot receive, because it neither sees Him nor knows Him; but you know Him, for He dwells with you and will be in you. I will not leave you orphans; I will come to you. John 14:16-18 NKJ

Nevertheless I tell you the truth. It is to your advantage that I go away; for if I do not go away, the Helper will not come to you; but if I depart, I will send Him to you. John 16:7 NKJ

"But when the Helper comes, whom I shall send to you from the Father, the Spirit of truth who proceeds from the Father, He will testify of Me. John 15:26 NKJ

Who Is The Holy Spirit?

The Holy Spirit is the third Person of the Trinity of God. It is difficult for humans to understand how there can be only one God, as the Scriptures teaches, yet He can reveal Himself as three persons. So do not let it be an obstacle for you. The Holy Spirit is a person, not just a force. He should be treated with the utmost respect and given the utmost gratitude.

How Does The Holy Spirit Help You?

Following are a few of the ways the Holy Spirit desires to help you recognize your announcer, and will help you if you allow Him to.

In Prayer

Likewise the Spirit also helps in our weaknesses. For we do not know what we should pray for as we ought, but the Spirit Himself makes intercession for us with groanings which cannot be uttered. Romans 8:26 NKJ (There some prayer at the end of this book, pray them in The Holy Ghost)

But you, beloved, building yourselves up on your most holy faith, praying in the Holy Spirit, Jude 1:20 NKJ

One weakness of humans, compared to God, is in our limited knowledge. We do not even know what is happening on the other side of a wall, let alone the other side of the country. We also do not know what people are planning to do, but the Holy Spirit knows everything. And He will help us to pray accurately and effectively.

One way the Holy Spirit helps us in prayer is by giving us utterance in a language for prayer which we have never learned. Thus we can bypass our minds with their doubt and lack of understanding of what is best, and pray according to the perfect will of God. Wherever you need an announcer to recognize you is it in your career, business, choice of spouse, ministry pray in that direction. God is near always.

Guides Us

The Holy Spirit will, if allowed, guide you in every area of life; from the words you should speak to your announcer, to the choice of the spouse you should marry, to the investments you should make.

For as many as are led by the Spirit of God, these are sons of God. Romans 8:14 NKJ

Now when they had gone through Phrygia and the region of Galatia, they were forbidden by the Holy Spirit to preach the word in Asia. After they had come to Mysia, they tried to go into Bithynia, but the Spirit did not permit them. Acts 16:6-7 NKJ

"However, when He, the Spirit of truth, has come, He will guide you. John 16:13 NKJ . . .

Teaches Us All Things

"But the Helper, the Holy Spirit, whom the Father will send in My name, He will teach you all things . . . John 14:26 NKJ

Tells Us Things To Come. The Holy Spirit can even tell you your announcer in advance.

"However, when He, the Spirit of truth, has come, . . . He will tell you things to come. John 16:13 NKJ

CHAPTER SIX

EVEN WHERE YOU ARE NOW . . .

Where you are is not far from God at all. He can reach you there. All He needs to do is to announce your destiny through somebody. The good thing about God is that He is not short of people to use. If men refuse to be used by the Lord, God is amazingly capable of transforming stones to be used. He is more than able to locate you. There is no place too far away for Him to perform His wonder.

You may or may not be there when your announcer of destiny takes on the divine duty. David's announcer of destiny was not there when the servant made mention of him to King Saul. From the day the announcement was made, David's preparation began fully for his future enthronement. If God could locate David in the wilderness when he did not even expect it, He is able to locate you even where you are now.

Starting from the time he was to be announced by Samuel, to the time King Saul needed somebody to play for him, grace traced David to the wilderness where he was occupied with his assignment.

> And Samuel said to Jesse, Are all the young here? Then he said, <u>There remains yet the youngest, and there he is, keeping the sheep.</u> And Samuel said to Jesse, Send and bring him for we will not sit down till he comes here. So he sent and brought him in. Now he was ruddy, with bright eyes, and good looking. And the Lord said, Arise, anoint him; for this is the one. Then Samuel took the horn of oil and anointed him in the midst of his brothers; and the spirit of the Lord came upon David from that day forward. So Samuel arose and went to Ramah. (1 Samuel 16: 11-13)

Saul was suffering from the spirit of madness from the Lord and he needed a player to play with anointed hands. However, David was in the wilderness when he was mentioned. He was not in the palace, yet his name was mentioned before the king.

> Then one of the servants answered and said, Look, I have seen a son of Jesse, the Bethlehemite, who is skilful in playing, a mighty man of valour, a man of war, prudent in speech, and a handsome person; and the Lord is with him. (1 Samuel 16: 18)

Don't bother to transfer yourself from where you are. Even where you are now, God is able to stretch His hands of grace and glory upon your life to bring you to the limelight.

Joseph was not only in the prison, he was right in the dungeon of the prison. He had done nothing to be there. Somebody lied against him, and yet the Lord visited him in the dungeon. What is important is for God to be with you wherever you are. His memory is very sharp, and He can never abandon you there. He has His set time for you.

Human beings may forget you just as the chief butler did not remember Joseph, but God that created him did not forget. When the time of Joseph's manifestation came, the Lord prompted the same butler to announce Joseph's destiny.

The way God arranged for Joseph's announcer of destiny to arise was by giving Pharaoh a troubling dream. By reason of the troubling dream, the butler was prompted and Joseph was remembered even in the dungeon. Initially, Joseph wanted to help himself out, but it was impossible.

> But remember me when it is well with you, and please show kindness to me; make mention of me to Pharaoh, and get me out of this house. For indeed I was stolen away from the land of the Hebrews; and also I have done nothing here that they should put me into the dungeon. (Genesis 40: 14-15)

Verse 23 then says, "Yet the chief butler did not remember Joseph, but forgot him." The chief butler forgot Joseph because it was not yet time for him to announce Joseph's destiny. When it was God's time, it was in that same dungeon that God visited him and his destiny was announced.

> Then the chief butler spoke to Pharaoh, saying, I remember my faults this day. When Pharaoh was angry with his servants and put me in custody in the house of the captain of the guard, both me and the chief baker. We each had a dream in one night, he and I. Each of dreamed according to the interpretation of his own dream. Now there was a young Hebrew with us there, a servant of the captain of the guard. And we told him, and he interpreted our dreams to us; to each man he interpreted according to his dream. And it came to pass, just as he interpreted for us, so it happened. He restored me to my office and he hanged him. (Genesis 41: 9-13)

While all these announcements were going on, Joseph thought he was rotting away in the dungeon. He did not have any idea of what was being prepared for him. But within the twinkling of an eye, God's miraculous hands stretched to him in the dungeon.

> Then Pharaoh sent and called Joseph <u>and they brought him quickly out of the dungeon;</u> and he shaved, changed his clothing and came to Pharaoh. (Genesis 41: 14)

No matter what dungeon of life you may be in today, God's hands are long enough to pull you out victoriously.

> Behold, the Lord's hand is not shortened, that it cannot save; not His ear heavy that it cannot hear. (Isaiah 59: 1)

If He has asked you to stay where you are, just stay there and see how He is going to pull you out miraculously. It is all for His glory, and your destiny is going to be announced to give Him all the glory. Please note that even where you are now is not hidden from the Lord. He is going to announce you from there.

> Is not My word like a fire? says the Lord, and like a hammer that breaks the rock in pieces? (Jeremiah 23: 29)

IN CONCLUSION

ONCE YOUR DESTINY IS ANNOUNCED

"For I know the thoughts that I think towards," says the Lord. "Thoughts of peace and not of evil to give you a future and a hope."

There is an assurance that God is going to announce your destiny. He has promised you a future and a hope, and He is going to land you there safely. Once your destiny is announced, you must remain humble. You must never forget where God picked you up from. You must always remember that you have been brought to the kingdom for such a time as this.

Never forget to help the poor who are waiting to be announced. Always remember that you wouldn't have been where you are today if your announcer of destiny had ignored the prompting.

> Open your mouth for the speechless, in the cause of all who are appointed to die. Open your mouth, judge righteously, and plead the cause of the poor and needy. (Proverbs 31: 8a)

> I was eyes to the blind, and feet to the lame. I was a father to the needy; I took up the case of the stranger. I broke the fangs of the wicked and snatched the victims from their teeth. (Job 29: 15-17)

Once the burden and pains of life are taken from you, never forget to continue to love the Lord your God. Serve Him diligently and never let your head become too big so that your crown can fit in accurately.

As the Lord lives, you will enjoy your announced season of destiny. You will never be put to shame again in life. Nothing will pull you back to square one again in Jesus' name. Your appointed time will come, and affliction will never rise again in your life in Jesus' name.

> For man also does not know his time. (Ecclesiastes 9: 12a)

You may not know the time appointed to you, but once you know the owner of time, which is God Himself, He is going to guide you to discover the moment when your tears of sorrow are to be dried up in Jesus' name. You will never be put to shame.

PRAYER POINTS

1. Sin that would make me hide when You call, Father deliver me from it.

2. Sin that would drive me from Your presence, Lord let me not fall in it.

3. Jesus, let me not miss the opportunity for my destiny.

4. The challenges to my high place in life, I receive power in the name of Jesus to overcome.

5. Lord, remember Your promise and covenant upon my life, and take me from the land of slavery.

6. Father, bear my misery no more, but deliver me from the oppressor.

7. Lord, get the attention of my deliverer and let him or her remember their assessment for my life.

8. Lord, any fear or doubt that delays my helper, remove it that he/she may come for my help.

9. God, announce me as a child of authority in land of slavery and affliction for deliverance.

10. God, demonstrate Your power in my life with signs and wonders that enemies will be happy for my deliverance.

11. Lord, I refuse to leave Egypt empty-handed, by Your power.

12. Lord, assist and support me through the journey of my destiny.

13. Lord, by Your mercy let Your plans and purpose for my life be accomplished.

14. Lord, let the work of my enemies turn to my glorious adventure, and let their plans against me turn to foolishness.

15. Lord, as no one can cover the glory of sun, let know man or demon be able to cover my glory.

16. Lord, the gift you have given that will take me to my destiny, make it known to my announcer of destiny.

17. Father, the incident that will happen that will take me from the wilderness or the prison to the palace, Lord, make it happen.

18. Every spirit of forgetfulness over my announcer of destiny that makes me remain at the spot, the blood of Jesus is against you.

19. God, take me out from the room of forgetfulness and let the announcer of destiny remember me.

20. Lord, guard me through the journey of calling and destiny that enemies thought was my destruction.

21. Father, relocate and surround me with people that matter to my destiny.

22. Lord, before princes and princesses that matter to my destiny, let my name be mentioned.

23. In the name of Jesus, let the announcer of my destiny appear from the four corners the world to announce me.

24. Lord, put the solution of my enemies in my hand.

25. Every veil of envy, jealousy, or ignorance that covers up people who matter to my destiny, God remove it.

26. Let my announcer be at the right place at the right time because of me.

27. God, as your hand was heavy on Jonah to deliver the message to Nineveh, so let my announcer have no peace until he has discharged his duty concerning my destiny.

28. As Saul's father servant lead him to Samuel for his kingship, Lord, direct people who will lead me where my blessing is. God, bring them on my way.

29. Every hand to frustrate my effort, I command you to wither off.

30. Anyone that has seen me struggle but refuses to help, waiting for me to give up, Lord, disgrace them by raising help from the four corners of the world for me.

.